"They Are Always with Me"
(Marie Antoinette's Aria)
from *The Ghosts of Versailles*

John Corigliano

transcribed by Tellef Johnson

T0028136

* Play all tremolos as rapidly as possible (unmeasured).
** Use fingers with side of hand to produce clusters.
*** Repeat boxed figures and phrases,
    ad lib., for indicated duration.

They _____ are al - ways with me: _____

My cry - ing chil-dren, _____ The crowds_ push-ing_

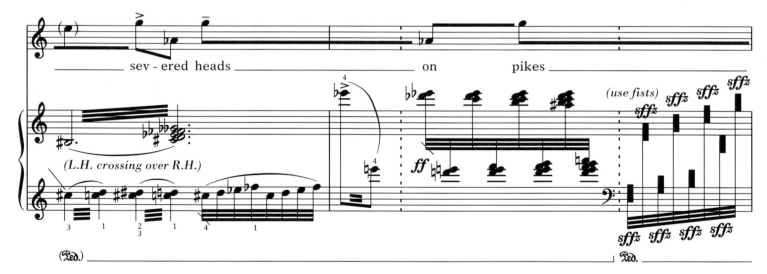

sev - ered heads _____ on pikes _____

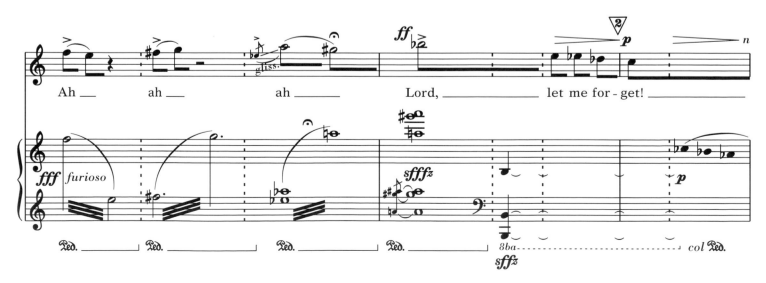

Ah __ ah __ ah _____ Lord, _____ let me for - get! _____

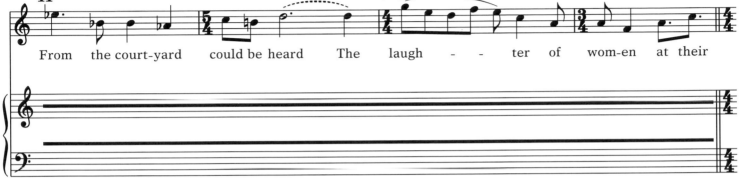

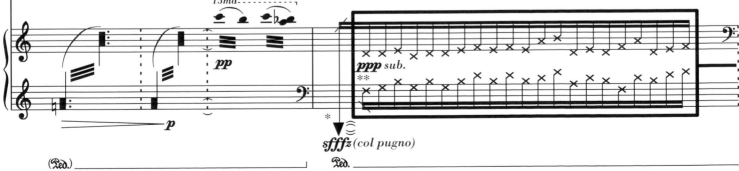

* ▼ designates lowest fist cluster (A-E).

** Fast, chromatic scampering, to be engulfed by the resounded fist cluster so that aura, not pitch, is important.

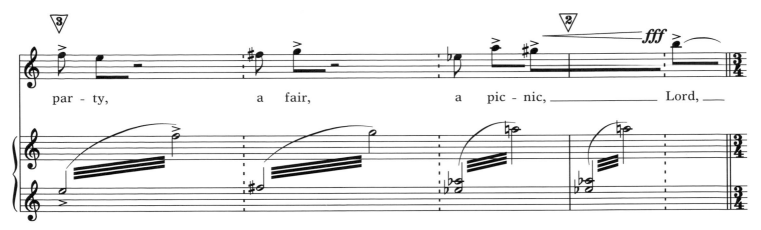

par - ty,　　　　a fair,　　　a pic - nic, _____ Lord, ___

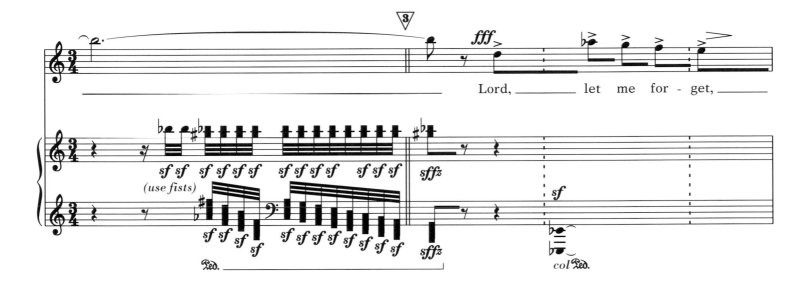

Lord, _____ let me for - get, _____

(use fists)

Ped. _____　　　col Ped.

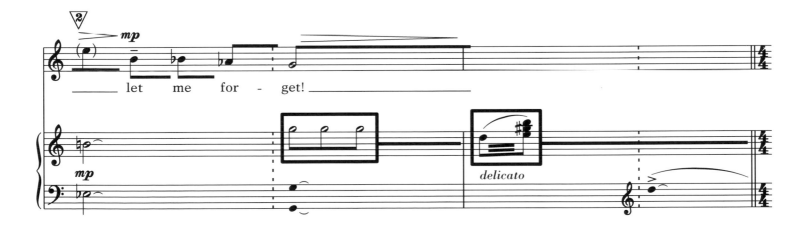

___ let me for - get! _____

delicato

♩ = 60

n < p

Once there was a gold - en bird   In

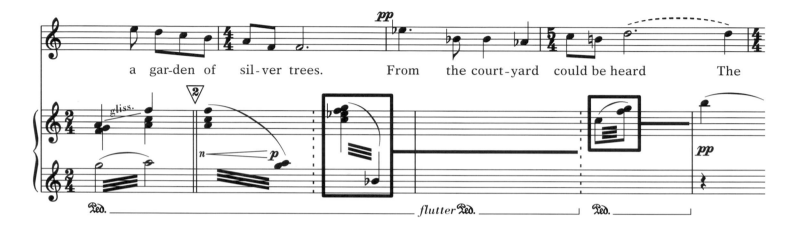

a gar-den of sil - ver trees.   From   the court-yard   could be heard   The

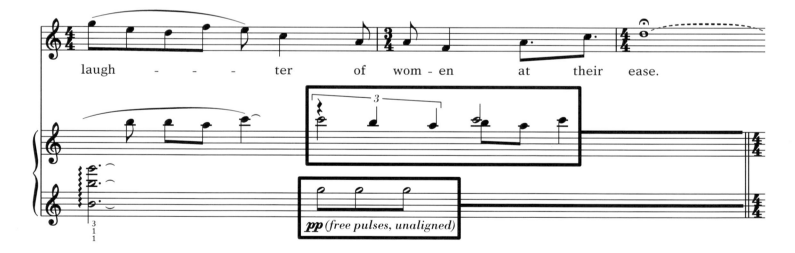

laugh - - - ter   of wom - en   at   their   ease.

Once   there was   a   gold-en bird   In ____

* Singer continues in time ($\frac{7}{8}$), ignoring conductor, who also continues in time ($\frac{4}{4}$), aligning with singer at the free beats ($\triangledown$).

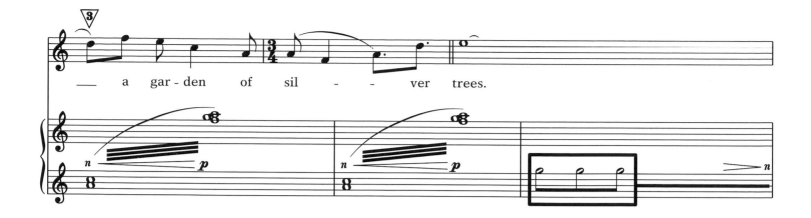

a gar - den of sil - - ver trees.

hazy

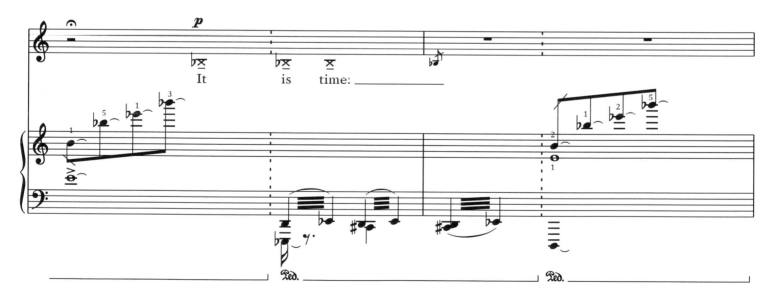

It is time: _____

weary

E - lev - en o' - clock. _____

"What will you eat?"___(t) they ask.___

"You will wear white,"___(t) they say.___

They cut my hair. They give me back my

ring. Am I go-ing to my wed-ding?___

(slowly lift up)----------- Ped.

The back of an ox-cart in the Oc - to - ber sun.

My peo-ple in-sult me, they scorn me, ___ they spit on me ___ as I ___ pass. ___

What are those flames? ___ Flags ___

___ in the streets of Saint Ho-no - ré. ___

* Keeping fingers on held chord, bring the palm down, smashing the remaining white notes in between.

What is that sound?

My fun-er-al drums. I climb the

stairs Am I dream-ing? Some-one a-wake me! Three steps. Four.

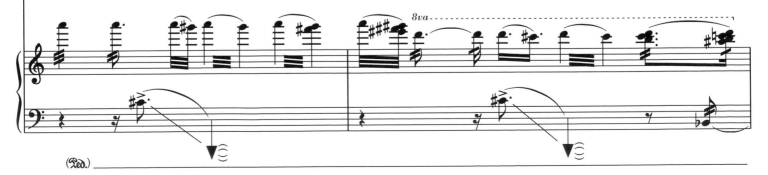

I want to cry out, I am in-no-cent,

in-no-cent! ___ Sev-en. _____ Eight. ___ Take

care _____ of my child-ren! Nine. Ten. Don't

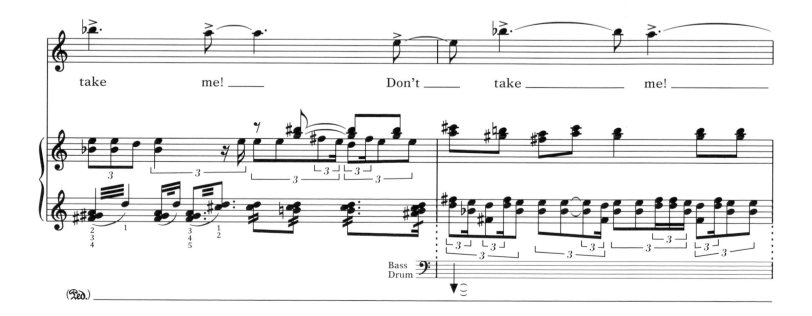

take ___ me! ___ Don't ___ take _____ me!

12

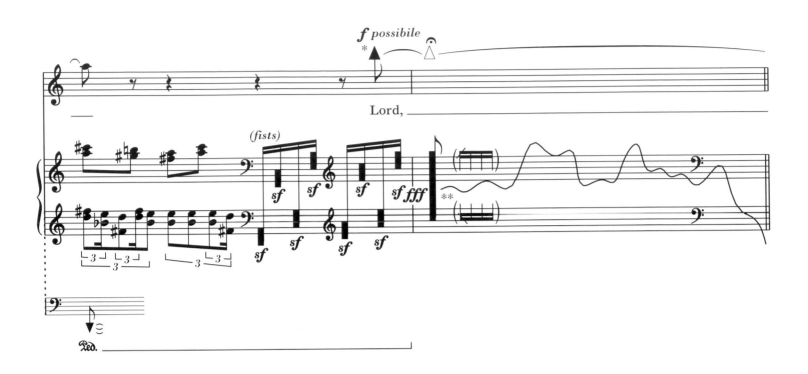

Lord,

Let me for - get, _____ let me for - get!

♩ = 60

Once

there was... _____

* Highest note possible.
** Lining R.H. and L.H. fists, careen down keyboard in parallel motion imitating contour given (in fast clusters).